FLASH,
CRASH,
RUMBLE,
and
ROLL

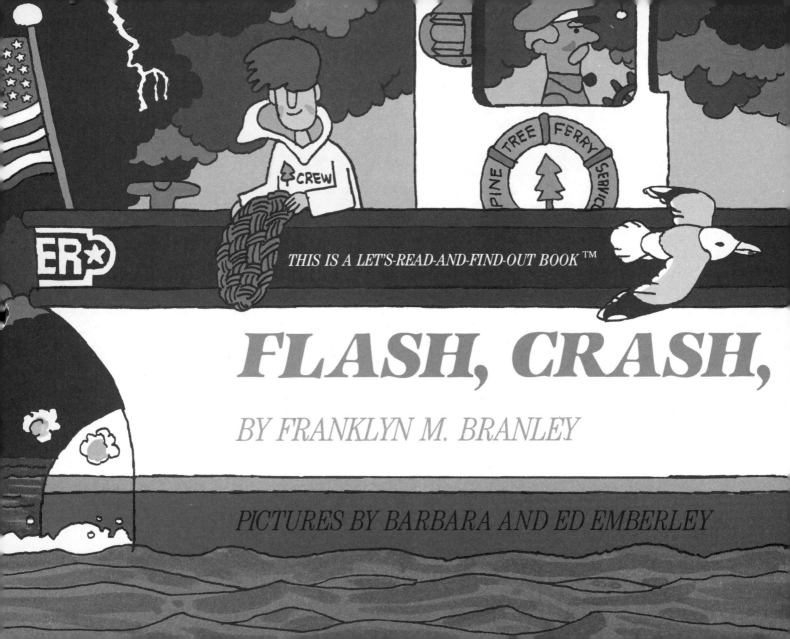

THIS IS A LET'S-READ-AND-FIND-OUT BOOK™

FLASH, CRASH,

BY FRANKLYN M. BRANLEY

PICTURES BY BARBARA AND ED EMBERLEY

RUMBLE, and ROLL

REVISED EDITION

A Harper Trophy Book

HARPER & ROW, PUBLISHERS

LET'S READ-AND-FIND-OUT BOOK CLUB EDITION

The *Let's-Read-and-Find-Out* series was originated by Dr. Franklyn M. Branley, Astronomer Emeritus and former Chairman of The American Museum-Hayden Planetarium, and was formerly co-edited by him and Dr. Roma Gans, Professor Emeritus of Childhood Education, Teachers College, Columbia University. Text and illustrations are checked for accuracy by an expert in the relevant field.

Published in hardcover by Thomas Y. Crowell, New York.
First Harper Trophy edition, 1985.

Flash, Crash, Rumble, and Roll
Text copyright © 1964, 1985 by Franklyn M. Branley
Illustrations copyright © 1985 by Ed Emberley

Library of Congress Cataloging in Publication Data
Branley, Franklyn Mansfield, 1915-
   Flash, crash, rumble, and roll.
   (Let's-read-and-find-out science book)
   Summary: Explains how and why a thunderstorm occurs
and gives safety steps to follow when lightning is flashing.
   1. Thunderstorms—Juvenile literature 2. Lightning
—Safety measures—Juvenile literature. [1. Thunder-
storms. 2.Lightning—Safety measures. 3. Safety]
I. Emberley, Barbara, ill. Emberley, Ed, ill.
III. Title IV Series
QC968.2.B73 1985B   551.5′54   84-45333
   (A Harper trophy book)
   (Let's-read-and-find-out books)
ISBN 0-06-445012-0 (pbk.)   84-48532

The day is quiet.
The air is still and hot.
Leaves do not move. Flowers droop.
Even the birds are still and quiet.

5

There are big white clouds in the sky.
They grow bigger and taller.
And they get darker and darker.

"Look at those black thunderclouds," people say.

"We're going to have a thunderstorm."

Warm air near the earth is rising into the clouds.

The air goes up fast.

Inside the clouds it keeps moving upward.

It may go all the way to the top and spill over.

The clouds keep growing.

After a while, the clouds may be ten miles high.

The rising air carries water. But it's not liquid.
It is a gas called water vapor.

When water vapor cools, it becomes liquid water.
That's what happens in the clouds to make them grow.
Water vapor cools and changes into small drops of
water, and also into small crystals of ice.

9

1

Air inside the cloud carries the water and ice up and up.

UP

2

The air gets colder and colder.

3

When it gets very cold, the air falls.

DOWN

4

So, inside a cloud, air is moving up very fast in some parts of it, and moving down in other parts.

WARM

COLD

Planes stay out of these dark thunderclouds.
The rushing air could turn a plane upside down.
It could even rip off the wings.

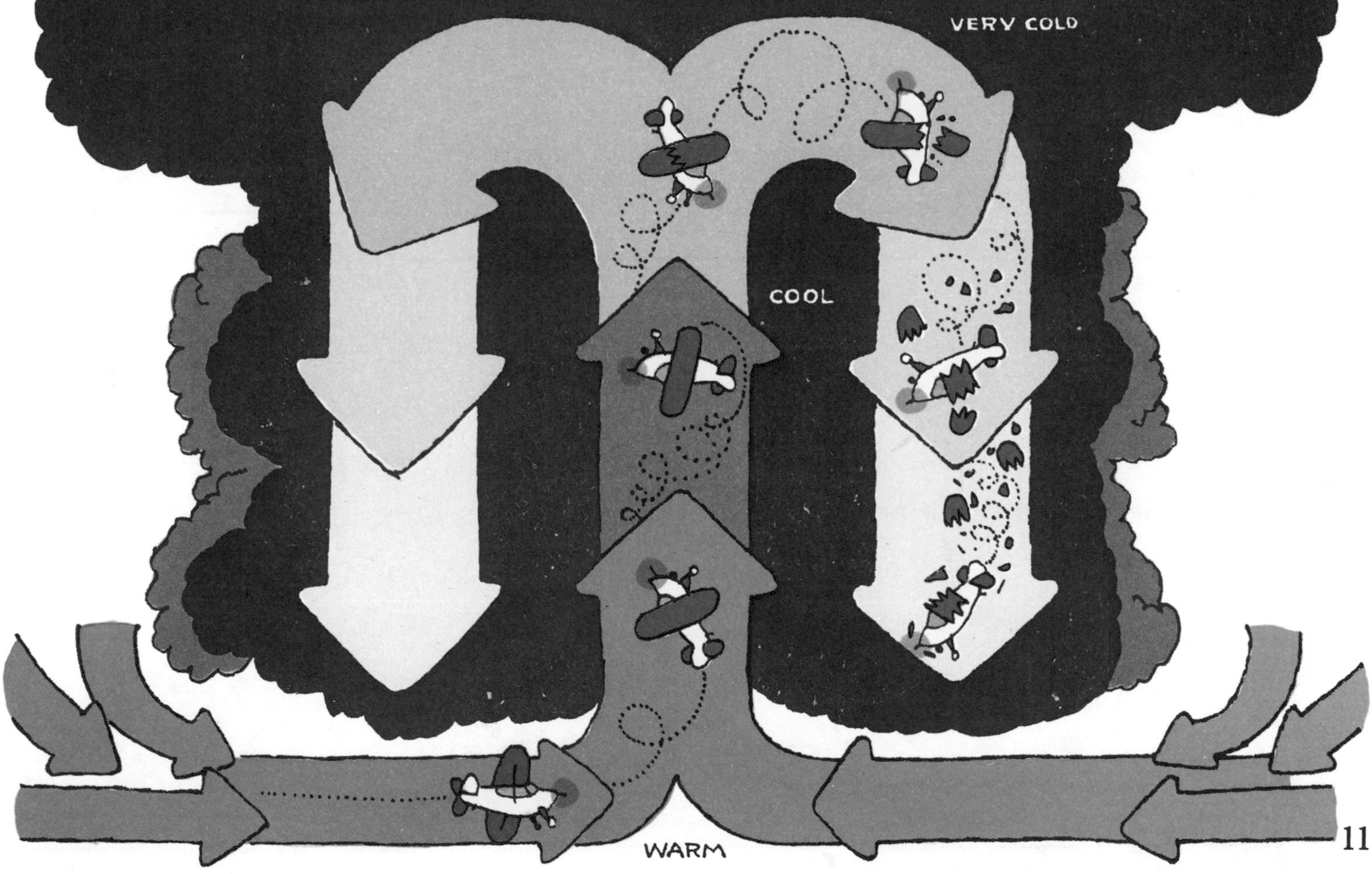

VERY COLD

COOL

WARM

Also, there's electricity in the clouds.
Each water droplet and ice crystal carries
a tiny bit of electricity.

There are billions and billions of droplets and crystals.
So the amount of electricity gets greater and greater.

When the amount is very great, the electricity jumps
from the top of the cloud to the bottom.
It makes a giant spark—a flash of lightning!

Rain starts to fall. First only a drop or two.

Then the wind blows, and the rain falls faster and harder.

Water races down the street. There's more lightning.

It may go from one cloud to another.

Or it may reach a high building or a tree.

The streak of lightning may be a mile long, or even longer.

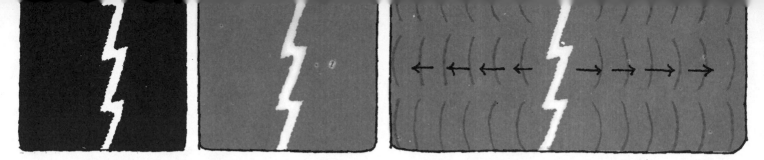

LIGHTNING . . . . . . HEATS THE AIR . . . . . THE HOT AIR EXPANDS, MAKING SOUND WAVES.

Thunder comes after the lightning.

The lightning is very hot. It heats the air. The hot air expands very fast.

It makes sound waves all along the streak of lightning.

→ COMING (QUIET) → → → CRASH !!! → → RUMBLE, RUMBLE → → → GOING (QUIET) → →

The sound waves reach you at different times.

When the first one reaches your ears there may be a loud crash.

As more and more sound waves reach you, the thunder rumbles and rolls.

16

You make sound waves when you break a balloon.

Blow one up and pop it.

The air in the balloon expanded rapidly through the break in the skin.

You made a tiny bit of thunder.

BANG!

There's only a little air in a balloon, so there's not much noise.

Lightning moves lots more air—billions of times more—

so there is lots of sound.

Sound waves travel slowly, much more slowly than the light from lightning.

Light travels so fast it can go to the moon in less than two seconds. It would take two weeks for sound to go that far.

Because light goes so fast, you see lightning the moment it flashes. But it may take several seconds for the thunder to reach you. It takes 5 seconds for the sound to travel 1 mile.

The next time you see lightning, try this:
Count the seconds until you hear the thunder.

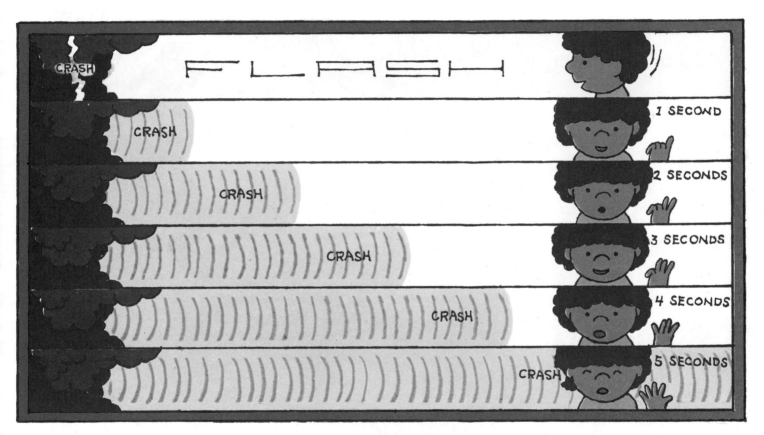

If 5 seconds go by, the storm is 1 mile away.
If 10 seconds pass, the storm is 2 miles away.
If only a second passes, the storm is very close.

The thunder will be very loud.
It may be scary,
but thunder won't hurt you.
  Lightning is different.

Lightning may start fires in houses or barns.
It may start forest fires. Lightning may knock over trees
and telephone poles. It may kill cows and horses in a field.
It may injure people or kill them.

You won't be hurt by lightning if you know what to do.

If you are swimming,
get out of the water.

If you are outside,
go inside.

If you are inside when a storm is close,

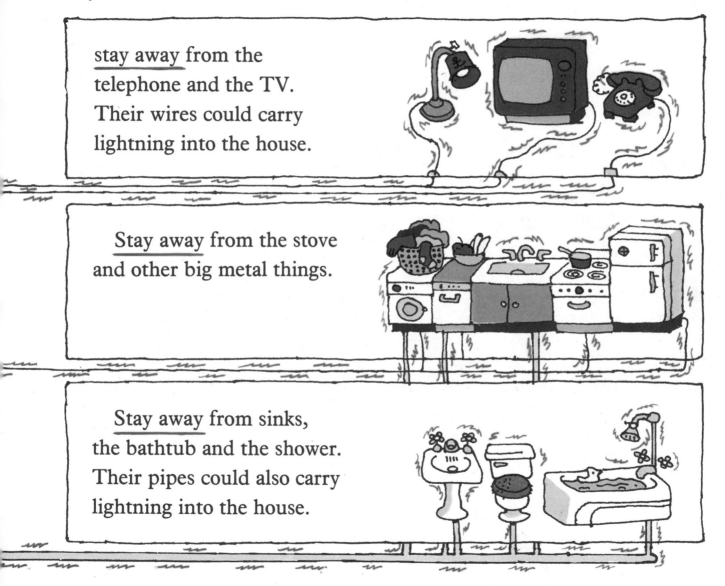

stay away from the
telephone and the TV.
Their wires could carry
lightning into the house.

Stay away from the stove
and other big metal things.

Stay away from sinks,
the bathtub and the shower.
Their pipes could also carry
lightning into the house.

If you are caught outdoors, keep away from a metal fence, or metal pipes. They could carry electricity.

Don't stand under a tree that is alone in a field.
Lightning usually strikes the highest thing. It might strike the tree.

So, if you're in a big field, don't be the highest thing around.
Crouch down, with your knees on the ground,
and bend your head forward.

If you are in a car, stay there.
A car is safe, because if lightning hits it
the electricity goes through the car
and not through you.

BEACH
DOCK
PICNIC
AREA

BACK
HOME
TOWN
CITY
CAMP

Watch the storm from a safe place. Before it begins, watch the clouds. You'll see them get bigger and bigger, taller and taller, darker and darker.

You'll see flashes of lightning. If the storm is far away, you'll hear thunder rumble and roll. If it's close by, the thunder will crackle and crash.

People used to think that lightning
was the fiery fingers of an angry god.
They thought the god made thunder
when he scolded and roared.

They feared storms as they feared their gods.

But there's no reason for us to fear storms.
We know what makes thunder and lightning.
And we know how to keep safe.

Franklyn M. Branley, Astronomer Emeritus and former Chairman of The American Museum–Hayden Planetarium, is well known as the author of many popular books about astronomy and other sciences for young people of all ages. He is also the originator of the Let's-Read-and-Find-Out Science Book series.

Dr. Branley holds degrees from New York University, Columbia University, and the State University of New York at New Paltz. He and his wife live in Sag Harbor, New York.

Ed Emberley is a graduate of the Massachusetts College of Art in Boston, and a writer and illustrator of many popular children's books, including ED EMBERLEY'S DRAWING BOOK OF ANIMALS. He and his wife, *Barbara Emberley,* have collaborated on several books, most notably DRUMMER HOFF, for which he won the Caldecott Medal in 1968. Mr. Emberley has illustrated other Let's-Read-and-Find-Out Science Books, including the original edition of FLASH, CRASH, RUMBLE, AND ROLL.

The Emberleys divide their time between the coast of Massachusetts and the mountains of New Hampshire, where they sail or ski in their spare time. Their children, Michael and Rebecca, have both written and illustrated children's books.